D0707917

FREE RUNNING

FIND YOUR WAY

Sébastien Foucan

Disclaimer
Freerunning can be dangerous, especially if undertaken without adequate training, preparation and having a high level of fitness. This book contains lifestyle advice only, and does not advocate or seek to promote any of the freerunning moves described or illustrated here. Neither the publisher nor the author can accept any responsibility for any consequences that may follow as a result of ignoring this advice.

FREERUNNING
FIND YOUR WAY

Sébastien Foucan

Michael O'Mara Books Limited

First published in Great Britain in 2008 by
Michael O'Mara Books Limited
9 Lion Yard
Tremadoc Road
London SW4 7NQ

Copyright © Sébastien Foucan 2008

www.foucan.com

The copyright in the images remains with the individual photographers.

All rights reserved. No part of this publication may be reproduced, stored in a retrieval system, or transmitted by any means, without the prior permission in writing of the publisher, nor be otherwise circulated in any form of binding or cover other than that in which it is published and without a similar condition including this condition being imposed on the subsequent purchaser.

A CIP catalogue record for this book is available from the British Library.

Papers used by Michael O'Mara Books Limited are natural, recyclable products made from wood grown in sustainable forests. The manufacturing processes conform to the environmental regulations of the country of origin.

ISBN: 978-1-84317-330-4

1 3 5 7 9 10 8 6 4 2

www.mombooks.com

Typeset and designed by Joanne Omigie

Printed and bound in Italy by L.E.G.O.

CONTENTS

PHOTOGRAPHIC ACKNOWLEDGEMENTS

The publisher and author would like to thank the following for permission to
reproduce their work within this book:

Susie Allnutt: p 9
Pete Dadds: p 36-7
Andy Day: pp 20-21, 92-3
Steve Downey and Scott Kellaway: pp 38, 46-7, 49, 55, 72-3, 86, 104, 105, 120, 121
Sébastien Foucan: pp 12-13, 30, 31, 40, 50-51, 64-5, 94, 126-7
Jamie Fry: pp 80-81
Martin Goodacre: p 19
Neale Haynes: pp 66-67, 114-15, 124
Jamie Kripke: pp 18, 48
Ola Kudu: pp 16-17, 26-7, 28, 41, 52-3, 60-61, 62-3, 68-9, 71, 84-5, 103, 108-9, 116-17, 118-19
Sandy Lund: pp 106-7
Paul O'Neill: pp 45, 78, 91, 100-101, 102, 110-11, 112-13
Alick Newman: pp 22-3, 29, 58, 59, 122-3
Platon: p 77
Igor Meijer: pp 24-5, 32-3, 34-5, 56-7, 82-3, 88, 89, 98-9
Brian Sweeney: pp 14-15

Every effort has been made to contact all copyright holders. Any omissions or errors that
may have occurred are inadvertent and will be addressed if notification is sent to the publisher.

ACKNOWLEDGEMENTS

I would like to thank my editor, Hannah Knowles, my agents, Sandy Lund and Clifford Bloxham, the Octagon Office, and the designer Joanne Omigie, who have helped to make this book happen (a long process!). Thanks also to Sarah Sandland for her publicity work.

Thank you to Michael O'Mara Books for believing in the project, and allowing me to make my dream come true.

To the Foucan family and my friends in France and the UK, and to all the people I have met along the way who have taught me life's lessons.

INTRODUCTION

MY NAME IS SÉBASTIEN FOUCAN.
I'm the founder of FREERUNNING and co-founder of Parkour.

My story began in Lisses, France, where as children my friends and I just followed our natural desire to run, jump and play; finding different ways of getting around our home town rather than walking on the pavements like everyone else. We'd jump on walls, through railings, across bollards . . . But whereas most people stop this kind of play as adults, we kept on doing it. We called this 'parkour', which means 'obstacle course'.

The discipline of freerunning developed when I started to evolve parkour to make it personal to the individual, so instead of being set moves, it could be adapted to suit each person's particular strengths and weaknesses. Doing this meant that the mental and physical aspects came together, and I could apply it to my own life and take lessons from my practice. From here, freerunning developed from a physical sport into an art.

There were three crucial moments in my life as a freerunner that helped bring what I do into the public eye: appearing in Mike Christie's two documentaries *Jump London* and *Jump Britain*; featuring in the Bond movie *Casino Royale* (*opposite*); and appearing with Madonna in the video for her single '**Jump**', and on her **Confessions World Tour**. Without these opportunities people might still not have heard of what I do, but now I can go around the world explaining the way of freerunning.

I think there is a different way for each individual. What is your way? Your way is who you are, what you dream of being, and what you would do if you knew you were going to die tomorrow.

Freerunning is the art of expressing yourself in your environment without limitations: it is the art of movement and action. For me, action is the most important thing in life. People who 'do' live their lives to the full; the rest just talk about it. My way is not about performing – it is simply the physical expression of being at one with your body and your mind.

In freerunning, as in life, it is always the obstacles that determine who you are. Learn how to overcome them, and you will never have to worry about anything. As adults we are afraid of obstacles and we live in competition with each other. We don't compare one baby to another, we just let them grow up according to their own rhythm. So why do we do this to each other as adults? Because our society says we should? I don't think we should follow that path.

Freerunning is an art that allows people to grow physically and spiritually according to their own paths, not society's.

I am not a master: I am still a student who is looking for his path. But I can see my way – and I'll keep following it until I've become all that I can be.

PART 1

FIRST STEPS

FREERUNNING IS AN ATTITUDE

. . . like using stairs instead of taking the lift, or walking rather than taking your car. I realize that what I do is not for everyone, but anyone can do freerunning if they want to, or at least have an experience of it – even if it's only jumping up stairs instead of walking. Remember, the way we move is just a routine that we've learned over centuries – we're not actually bound by walking in a certain way. So let's experiment and keep evolving.

THE FIRST STEP DOES NOT COMMIT YOU TO ANYTHING

When you are learning something, the first obstacle is thinking that everything you do is irreversible and that one step will commit you to a certain path. Go! Take one step, see for yourself how it feels, and the decision is yours as to whether you continue along that route – there are no obligations. I have fears just like everyone else, but without those first few steps and a little courage, freerunning would not exist.

POSSESSION IS ILLUSION

Nothing on this planet is permanent, and this is why I believe there can be no such thing as possession. Enjoy what you are doing because it might be the last time you do it – and don't attach your happiness and success to a specific person or place, because you have to continue to exist and thrive even when these are gone.

DON'T COMPETE

It's interesting to see how much people want to compete, to compare themselves with others, thinking that there's no other alternative if they are to make progress. Our society is highly competitive and everything we do is about being the best. The way of freerunning is different: freerunning is about constant evolution, it's not about victory or profits. Being a star, the best, the number one is a dream for a lot of people – when really what they need is to tell themselves they are OK as they are in the present moment, and that their achievements are amazing in their own right, without being compared to anyone else's.

In freerunning, competition is a limitation and an illusion: if your motivation is wanting to win a trophy, or to beat someone, you aren't thinking about what's best for you and your body. Focusing on what people think, rather than concentrating on your own way of expressing yourself, prevents you from enjoying the here and now.

Children learn quicker than adults, and I think it's because they focus on what they themselves are doing instead of on everyone else. They take inspiration from the world around them and progress every day at their own rhythm.

BE A PARTICIPANT

NOT A SPECTATOR

ENJOY THE
JOURNEY...

It is so much more than the destination. Your experience and what you learn as you travel through your life have more value than any goal you will ever achieve.

Destination is an illusion: you never know what is coming next, so try to live in the present moment – it really is all that matters.

When I feel stressed, the first thing I do is force myself not to walk away and ignore the problem, but instead tell myself that the problem is here and it won't go away until I accept it, deal with it, and move on. I find the best way for me to do this, and stay positive, is to keep focused on my work and stay in the present moment, remembering what I am good at instead of dwelling on negative things that have happened to me.

BE POSITIVE

In the modern world we are surrounded by stress and over-stimulated by sights and noises. We have to understand that to cope with this we need time to take our stress levels down, and just breathe. I believe that there is no situation, however bad, that lasts forever, and remembering that helps me get through the hard times.

DON'T WAIT
FOR THE RIGHT TIME

When I was younger I always thought there was a right time for doing things and I would wait for the moment when I was completely ready. But as I got older I realized that this 'right moment' doesn't exist: everything good that has happened to me has been unplanned, from *Jump London* and *Jump Britain* to *Casino Royale* and being on tour working for Madonna.

Nothing happens when and how you would really love it to – the right time is an illusion where we imagine everything will be perfect. When the best opportunities came to me I had tendonitis, felt unprepared, or tired, or had broken my wrist.

I don't wait for the right time any more, I just react to whatever comes along. The right time is just about taking opportunities. You have opportunities open to you every single day, so don't wait to seize them.

RESPECT YOUR ENVIRONMENT

The world is older than all of us, so learn from
it and respect it. Your environment is your
equipment, and unless you use it properly you will
harm it and yourself. The earth is precious to your
own development: treat it with care.

DON'T BE AFRAID
TO BE AFRAID

I never try to act like I'm not afraid; instead I always try to face my fears. I don't like competition, but I do like a challenge. When I am freerunning I don't try to impress people or to show off – I do it for myself.

I actually hate working on high ground, and taking risks on rooftops: believe it or not I've actually got a bit of vertigo! But I believe in the power of the mind and in willing myself to do something, no matter how large the obstacles, or how much I might dislike the idea of doing it. I've learned from my experiences, but that doesn't stop me from constantly experimenting.

With time I've realized that fear is just my brain telling me that I have to be careful, and no more than that. Once I've calmed down, I can go on to achieve what I was afraid even to try.

EMBRACE DIFFERENCE

I learn from everything around me, not just the physical arts, and try not to be restricted by my own beliefs. I've been particularly inspired by Asian cultures, which are really focused on energy and the spirit: in particular the Japanese martial art Aikido, which teaches the concept of harmony and how to react to someone else's actions, and the Indian art of yoga, which teaches that energy is linked to your body and demonstrates the purifying qualities of proper breathing.

Indigenous tribes are really connected with their environment: climbing trees, wearing few clothes, walking barefoot and practising body breathing. There's a good reason why some of these practices have been around for thousands of years: they still work, and they work because they're natural.

The freerunning way is to be like a sponge and absorb from other cultures. By doing this, and not being worried if someone does things differently from us, we can evolve.

DON'T TAKE LIFE TOO SERIOUSLY

Having a serious attitude when you're doing something doesn't mean that you're good at it or that you're being professional. It's OK to enjoy what you're doing and to laugh while you're doing it; it helps to be relaxed.

IT'S CHILD'S PLAY

The world is your playground – enjoy it! Remember: freerunning started as children playing, so think like a child and enjoy how you move.

PART 2

TRY, TRY AGAIN

UNLEARN WHAT YOU HAVE LEARNED

MENDELSSOHN'S
TREE
See wall plaque for details!

Every day, people say things like (and you might recognize yourself here): 'I'm too old', 'I'm too young', 'I can't because…', 'He/She is better than me', 'I'd love to do it but…', 'I don't have time'.

By saying these things, we programme ourselves with hundreds of excuses. This is a quick example of conditioning, but there are lots of other examples: the way we walk, talk, interact etc. To follow my way and to develop freerunning I had to unlearn things every day and fight against this conditioning, to stop myself thinking 'I can't do this' or 'I can't do that'. It's harder to unlearn things than it is to learn them, but it is by doing this, and by breaking cycles of behaviour, that you will really come to understand your true self – and not the person the world around you has told you to be.

Life is about movement and rhythm – but you will only find your own personal rhythm by listening to your body and by practising what you do until you can do it without thinking.

ALWAYS PRACTISE

Most of the answers to the questions in my life have come to me through action – it is when I stop moving that life becomes difficult to comprehend. It took me years to feel completely natural in my freerunning, and it's interesting to see how fast you lose your innate feeling for something when you stop doing it for a while. The secret is to keep moving and keep the energy flowing. The energy has to keep circulating, because movement is life.

LISTEN TO YOUR BODY – IT KNOWS BEST

No one knows my body better than me, because I listen to what it is telling me. Doctors and physiotherapists always ask you how you are feeling and to describe the pain you have because only you are in the best position to know what is happening to your body – so don't shut yourself off to the signals it gives you. If you ignore it, don't be surprised when you start to suffer pain and injuries.

After nineteen years of freerunning, I have developed a special sensitivity to my body, so when I feel pain I automatically adapt my practising or stop if I know it is too much for my body to take.

When I was young the other kids didn't really look at me. Most of the time they'd think I wasn't interesting or I was wasting time on something pointless when I was doing parkour. I was shy and not really confident, and the fact that I wasn't tall and always looked younger than my age didn't help. I never liked being the one taking the lead or taking risks, but with time, lots of practice and sacrifices, a refusal to give up, and by keeping focused on my dream, I started to achieve things that I never thought I would be able to.

TRY, TRY AGAIN

So remember: it is normal not to be able to do something the first time you attempt it. Whether it's something in your work or in your exercise that you're struggling with, keep trying; do it again, but set the bar a bit lower this time and only raise it gradually when you're ready. Remember how many times you needed to attempt it before you succeeded, then do it again and again – repeat the action like a wave that keeps coming to the shore. Gradually you'll do it in fewer attempts, then one day, eventually, you will do it in one.

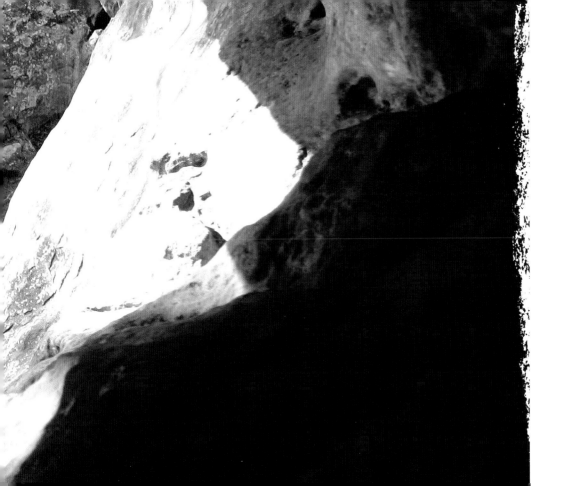

FOLLOW YOUR INSTINCT, NOT OTHER PEOPLE

LEARN FROM OTHER DISCIPLINES

Feel free to try other disciplines: experience is everything, so avoid being restricted by one idea or place. When we are young we will try almost anything because we love experimenting with new experiences. As we get older we stop trying to learn different things because we think we know enough – but you can never know enough, and you can always learn from other crafts.

I used to be a firefighter in Paris, which was a job that required huge discipline and entailed taking on massive responsibilities. When I changed my path to pursue freerunning as an art, I carried with me the self-discipline I'd learned from firefighting to help me become the best that I could be.

There is always something for me to learn from as a freerunner, whether it's football, tennis, athletics, gymnastics or dancing and other performing arts. Being on stage with Madonna, for example, has given me the opportunity to see how she manages herself under pressure, and also to appreciate the dancers' skills and the way they adapt themselves to absorb new moves that the choreographers teach them. It was interesting to see how many similarities there are between what they do and my own art, and it showed me that every discipline has something specific that you can learn from.

WHAT IS TRUE TODAY WON'T BE TRUE TOMORROW

When I was a firefighter, I was chosen to be a part of the special gymnastic team and to start to plan my future training in the team. The day after I was chosen, I broke my arm in a serious accident and almost lost it. I had to train for almost a year to regain the capacity to move my arm properly. This moment changed my perception of life completely.

I take nothing for granted now and don't harbour regret for what might have been. If it hadn't been for that accident I might not be where I am today, or have had such incredible experiences. Even when it seems your life is mapped out, tomorrow it will change in a way you never expected.

LESS IS MORE

In freerunning, more does not mean better. It is not about how high or how far you can jump, or trying to do the most spectacular moves. It is about naturally relating your body to your environment and exploring yourself and the world around you. It is often in the smallest and slowest movements that we appreciate this most.

ALWAYS READ

It's easy to forget that even after we leave school we never actually stop learning, right up until we die.

My inspiration for freerunning never stops and often comes from various books I've read: I love *Jonathan Livingston Seagull* by Richard Bach, with its tale of non-conformity and striving for self-fulfilment; *Tao of Jeet Kune Do* by Bruce Lee inspired me, because it helped me to see I could extend my discipline on to a more philosophical level; Dan Millman's *Way of the Peaceful Warrior* really captured for me everything I am trying to achieve with freerunning and it made me feel that there is no secret to this planet – everything you discover has already been seen or done by someone else. Whatever your mood, whatever your situation, you can always find a book that will inspire you and help you find your way.

TAKE A DIFFERENT PATH

You gain much from leaving the well-worn road: you must give up your sense of security and there are always risks, but to find your own path is essential to your growth as a human being. It takes time to be sure of your personal tastes and choices; everyone has a different rhythm, whether it's in the small things, for example a preference for a particular colour or tune, or in more fundamental things, such as what job we choose. Being different is often to appear to reject being with everyone else, but it isn't rejecting their way – it's looking for your own.

ALWAYS DO YOUR BEST

AND YOU WILL NEVER DISAPPOINT YOURSELF

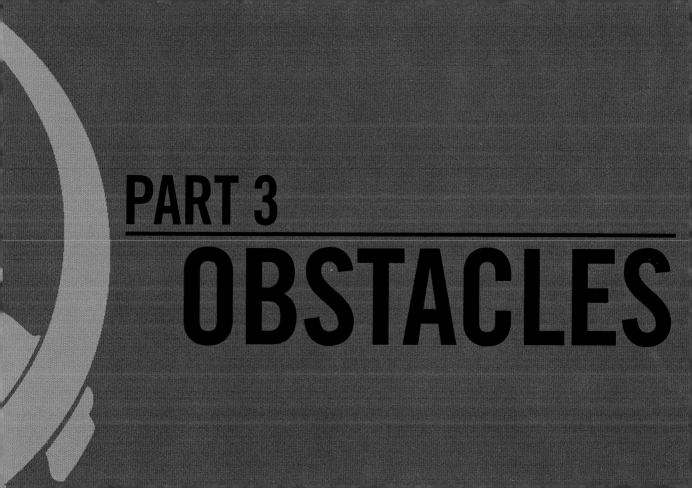

PART 3
OBSTACLES

THE OBSTACLES YOU FACE WILL DEFINE YOU

Obstacles are enemies that can take many forms: physical, mental, social… When your momentum is halted by an obstacle, you are forced to face your fear. How you respond to that fear is what will make you who you are. Will you turn around and go back the way you came? Or will you work out how to overcome it?

Freerunning is about realizing that obstacles are a part of your pathway, and you can apply the same philosophy to your everyday life. Obstacles and difficulties make you stronger when you decide to face them. And remember: there is always something to learn from successes *and* failures.

WALLS AREN'T ALWAYS BARRIERS

THERE ARE RISKS EVERYWHERE

Where one person sees a potential fall, I see a potential flight. Preparation is always the key to every good action. To remain within your comfort zone is an option, but don't then hope to rise to great heights. The successful path is rarely the easiest or most comfortable: to make progress is always difficult. Life involves lots of risk-taking and it will always be a succession of challenges, but don't be afraid to lose! It is only by tasting the bitterness of your mistakes that you will enjoy the sweetness of your achievements.

WHEN YOU'RE DOING SOMETHING DIFFERENT YOU ARE ALONE MOST OF THE TIME

But that doesn't mean that you can't find people to share ideas with along your journey. Travel together and help each other to grow, but don't alter your path just so you have company.

KNOW YOUR LIMITS

I understand my skills and know how to use them properly because I know what my limits are. Understanding how much is too much gives me the confidence and freedom to explore all possibilities that *are* within my capacity. I don't waste time putting pressure on myself to do things that I know are physically or mentally beyond me – I like to think that one day I will be able to do them, but if it isn't to be today it doesn't bother me.

If you keep asking for assistance in what you do, don't be surprised if you lose your strength and your confidence. Permanent protection from risk is a state no better than stagnation: it is only through making your own mistakes and taking your own risks that you will truly gain self-awareness.

Before I started to develop freerunning, I tried to find teachers or masters to help me. Later, I realized that my mistake was not believing that I had all the knowledge and the capacity in myself and in the world around me to tackle my problems. So I tried to develop the ability to find the solution to my problems by myself. I'm sure if I'd relied on someone else to help me I would have taken a lot longer to achieve what I have, and I would not understand myself nearly so well.

When I was kid, a friend, who I will call by his nickname, 'Kamikaze', said to me: 'The problem with your generation is that you've got everything – computers, the internet, books, TVs, DVDs, etc. – but you still ask how to do things. When I was young we always found a solution in ourselves and asked ourselves – how does it work?'

DON'T ALWAYS ASK FOR HELP

Injury is the worst thing for a freerunner, but the necessary rest provides you with the time to gain perspective and to see yourself and what you do in the context of real life. I've had two major injuries – broken bones, though not from freerunning – at two different points in my life. Those frustrating moments turned into positive experiences because they gave me the opportunity to learn how to listen to my body, and how to have the mental strength and determination to recover.

THERE IS A TIME TO MOVE AND A TIME TO REST

KEEP MOVING FORWARD
NO MATTER WHAT OBSTACLES YOU FACE

PART 4
FREEDOM

ENERGY IS CONTAGIOUS –
CATCH IT AND PASS IT ON

BE FREE LIKE ANIMALS

Humans are animals: we've just forgotten how to move like we are. All things feline have influenced me immensely, by the way they move, but also by their way of life – simultaneously living on the margins of society while finding acceptance in it, which allows them great freedom.

PERFECTION DOESN'T EXIST

No one is perfect, and no one can achieve perfection. The only way is to find harmony: harmony with yourself and your environment. When I started freerunning, I found it hard to achieve what I wanted because there was always something wrong with what I was doing, and it annoyed me. I thought perfection was the most important thing to reach, but I came to realize that we don't have enough time on this earth to achieve perfection.

Because nothing is constant, we just have to find a harmony with our bodies and minds so we can react to change and do the best we possibly can. Finding harmony within yourself really is an art and it requires a lot of discipline and time, but the rewards are endlesss.

YOUR WAY
HAS NO NAME

Freerunning is the name I chose to reflect my practice and the evolution of my art, but I don't restrict my way to the domain of physical movement: it's about living life as fully as possible, mentally, physically and spiritually – and this is why your way has no name, because no one word can encapsulate your journey.

Like Mr Keating in *Dead Poets Society*, who makes his pupils stand on their desks to see the world from a different perspective, I always try to put myself in different positions or on different levels to see the world from new viewpoints.

We should take time to appreciate our environment and not always look at it from the same places, the same angles. Change your perspective.

GOOD AND BAD DO NOT EXIST

'Good' and 'bad' are just different points of view. What is important is that you learn from your experiences, whether they make you laugh and smile, or cry and shout.

BE INSPIRED AND INSPIRATIONAL

I live by inspiration: it's a universal link connecting us all. Some people will give you inspiration and make you dream, and at the same time everything that you do in your life can be a positive inspiration to someone else.

I am inspired by many different people – Bruce Lee, Michael Jordan and Zinedine Zidane, for example, have all inspired me by the way they move and by their dedication to their talent. Sometimes, however, inspiration can come from more obscure things. For instance, I find watching how horse trainers prepare their animals before a race so instructive: whether it's making sure they have had a good morning run; or feeding them the right food; or in their understanding that each animal is different and that preparation must be tailored to the individual horse. This idea of tending to the individual is something I've applied in developing freerunning.

ONCE YOU'VE FOUND YOUR PATH, STAY TRUE TO IT

Throughout your life you have to navigate through currents of good times and bad – you can't control this. All you can do is stick to your course and maintain your position at the helm, no matter what comes your way.

I remember great moments in my life: having close friends, making good decisions, opportunities opening up for me, people listening to me, discovering fame and money and feeling strong and confident. But I also remember losing friends and money, having people ignore me, being disliked, making poor decisions, feeling jealousy, being criticized by others, having injuries, and feeling tired and vulnerable. All these moments – the good and the bad – only improved my strength and determination to keep to my own path, as they should for you too.

WE GO IN SEARCH OF OURSELVES OUR WHOLE LIVES

YOUR LIFE AS A ROAD
YOUR FEELING AS A GUIDE
YOUR BODY AS A VEHICLE